Kawaii Princess
Coloring book

Vibrant
Visions
Publishing

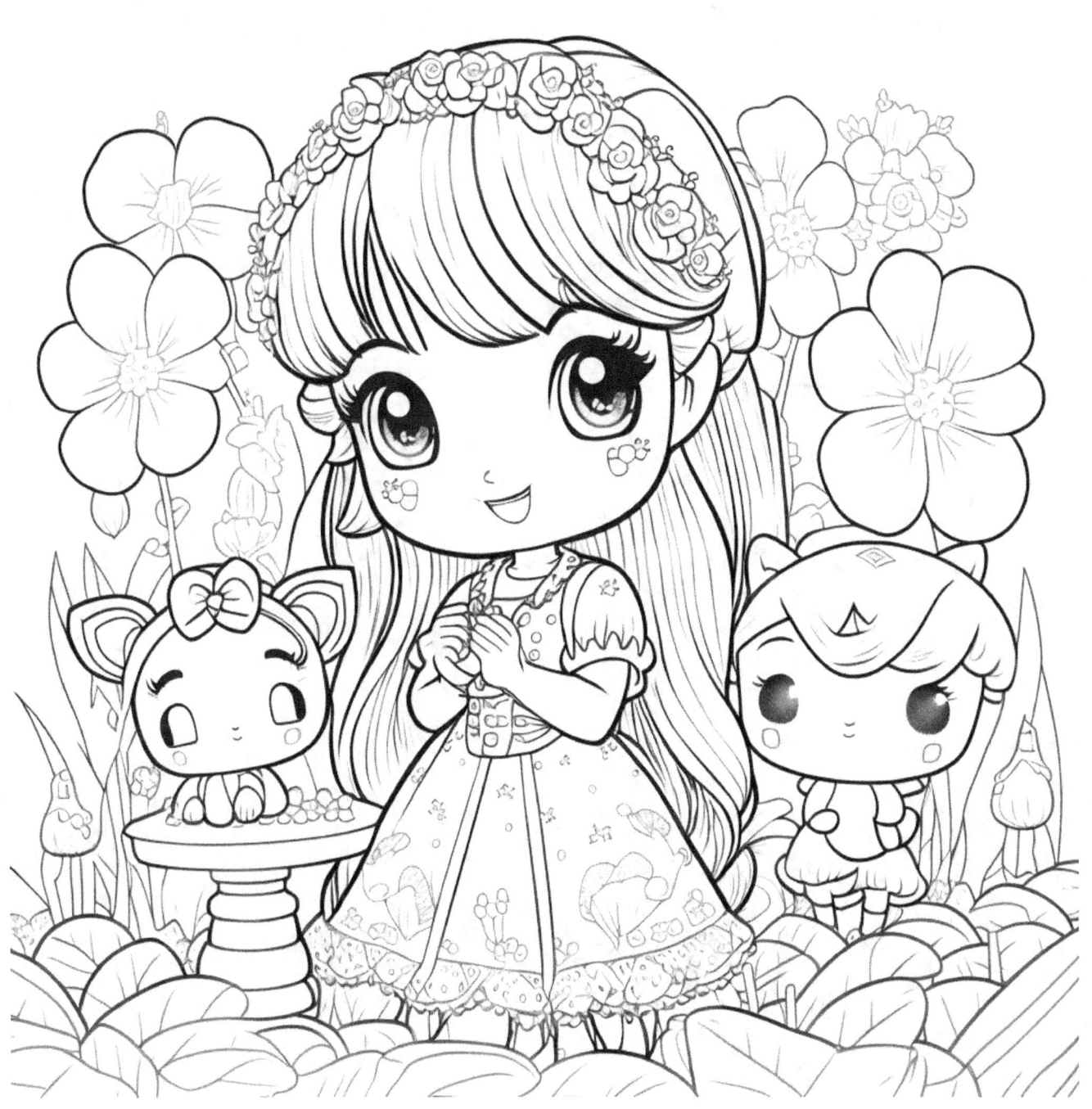

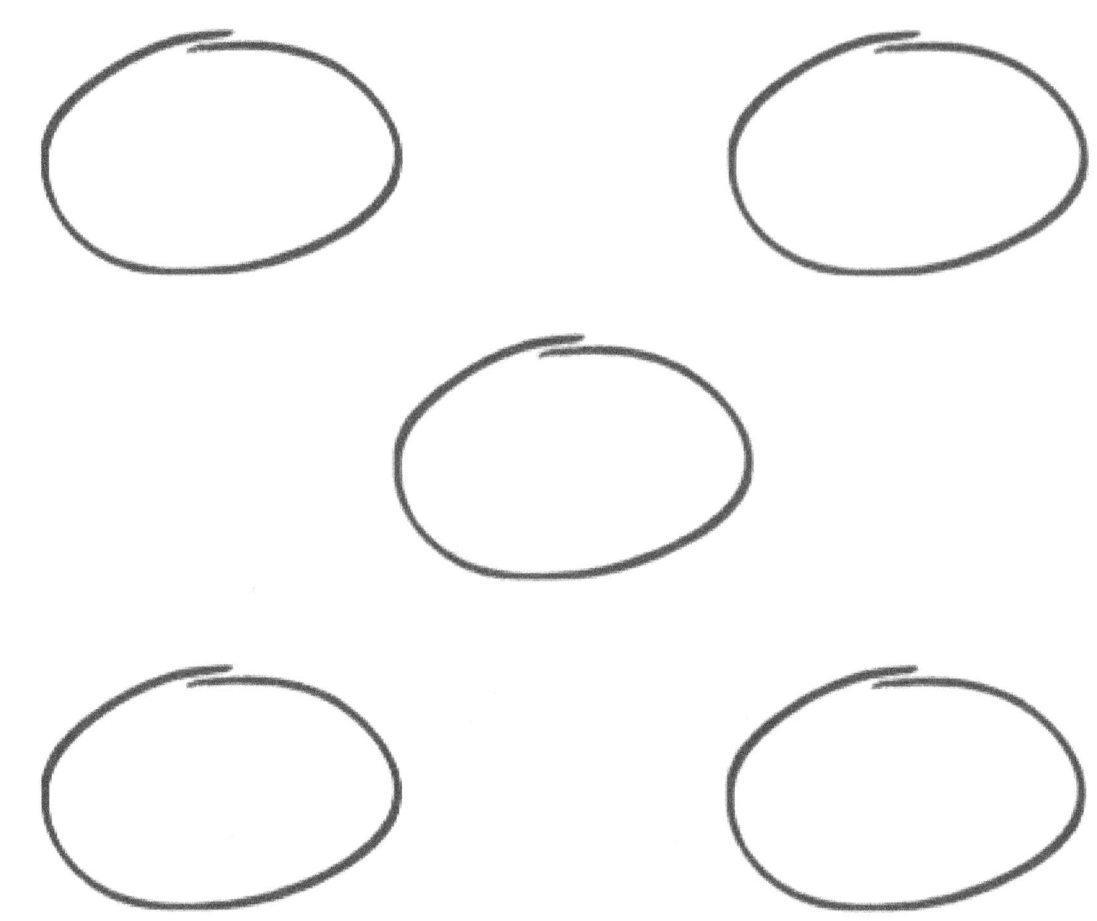

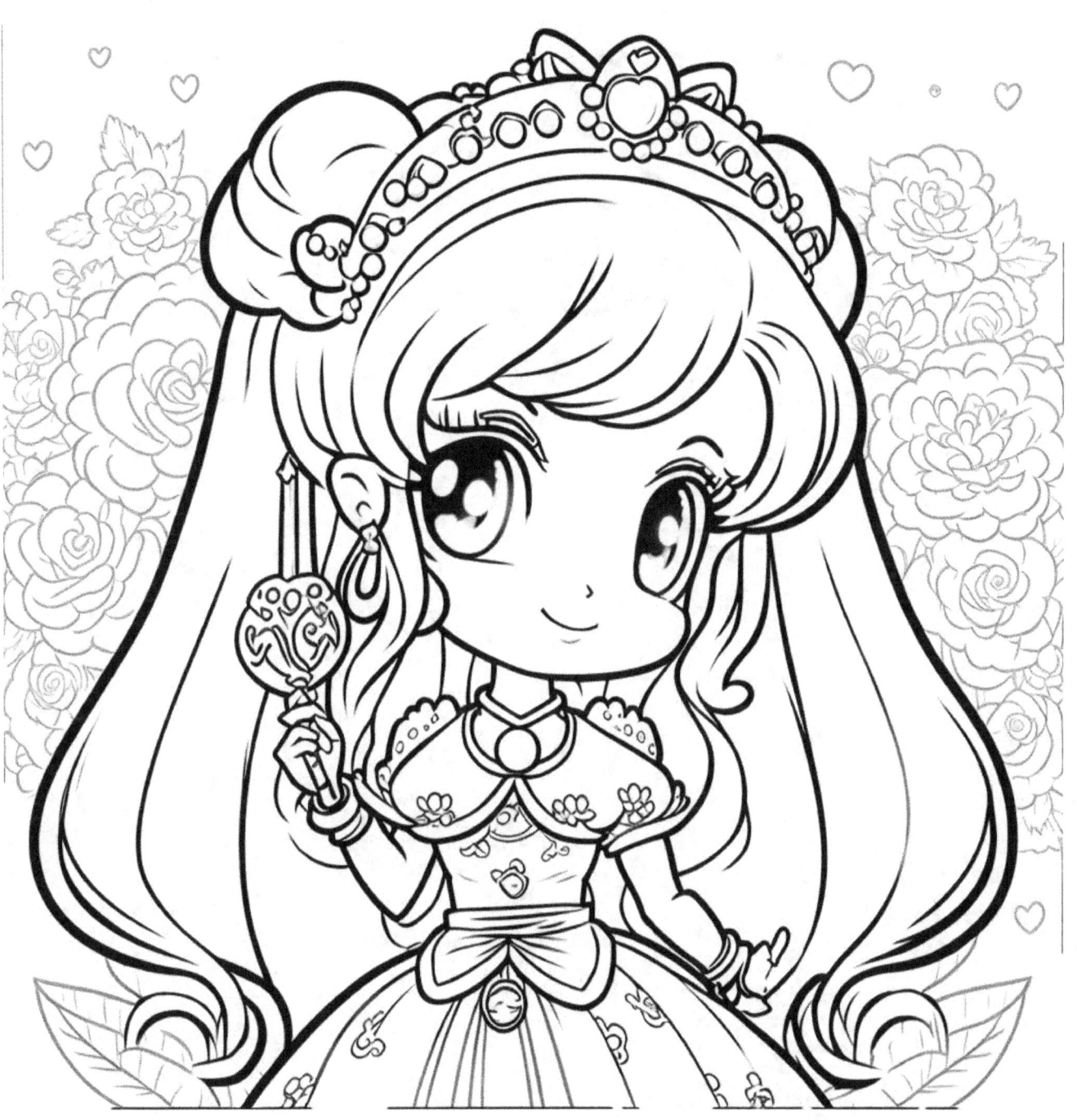

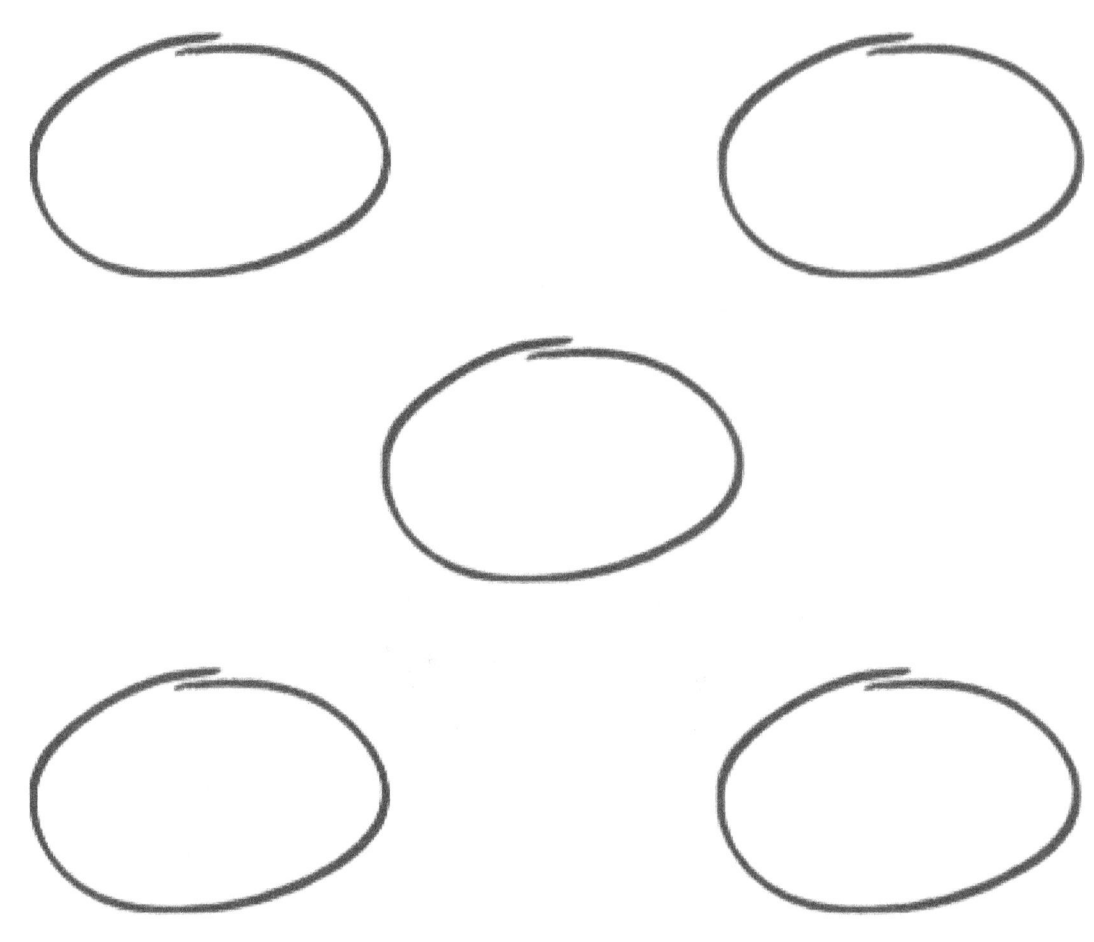

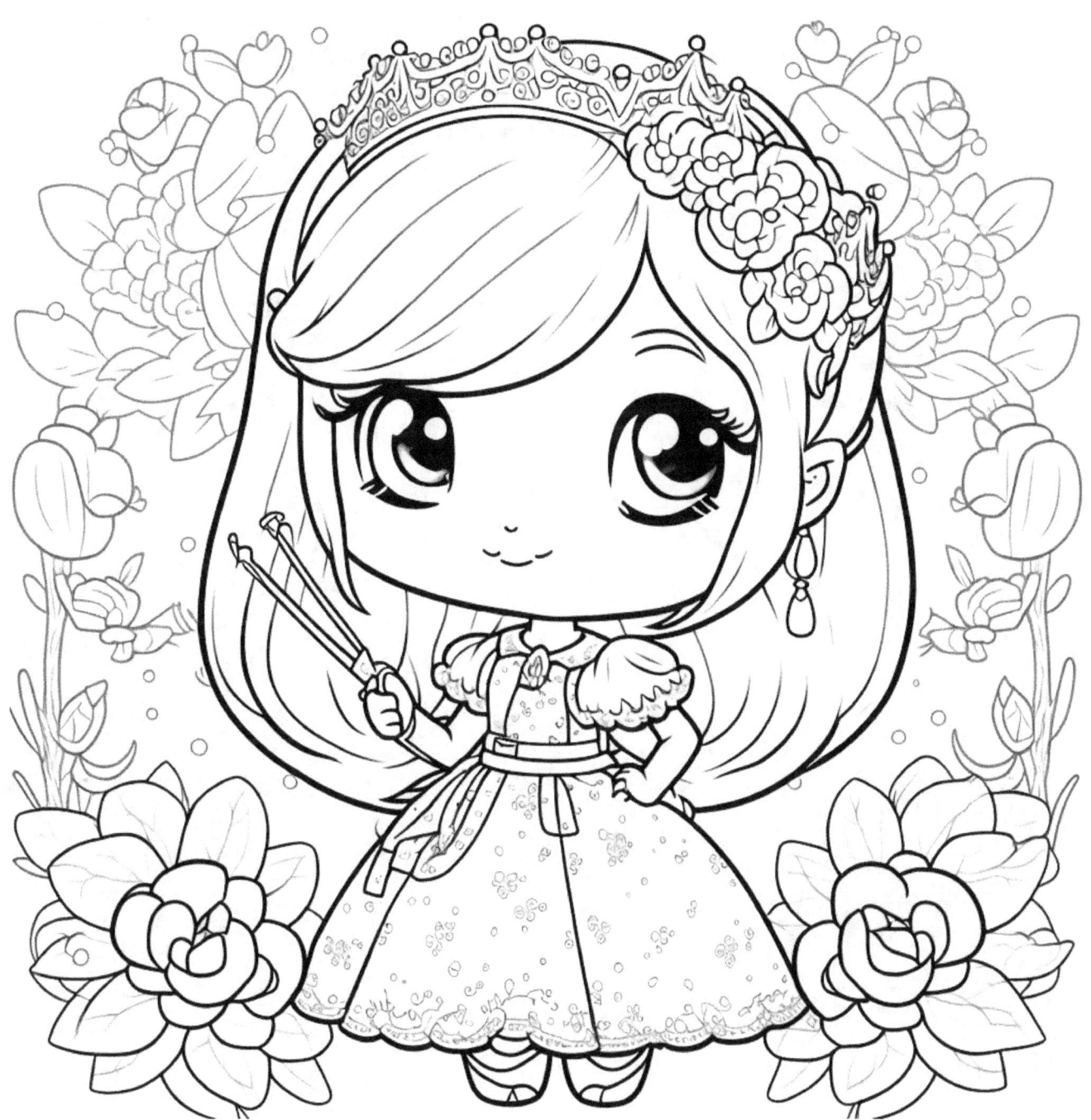

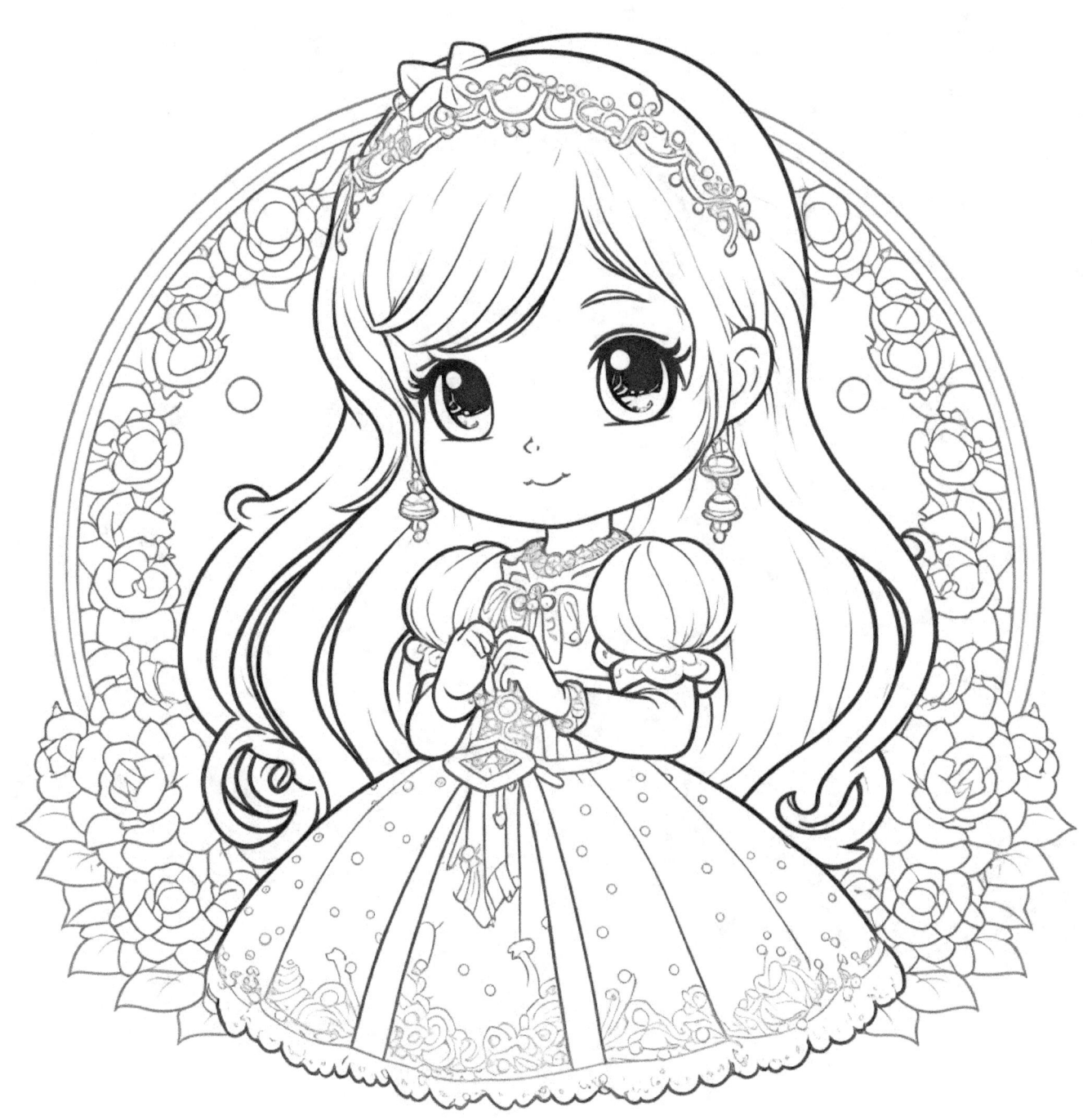

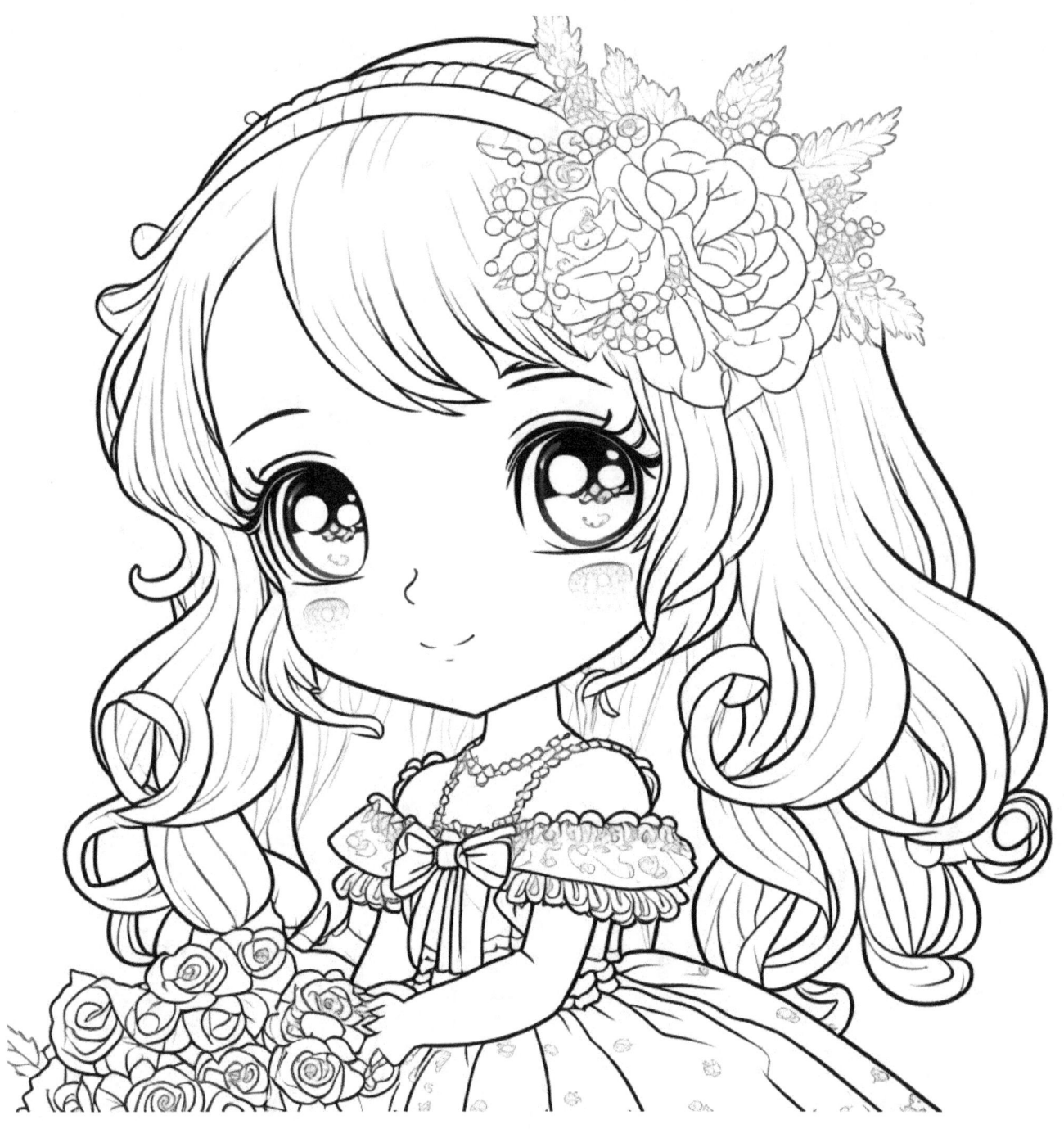

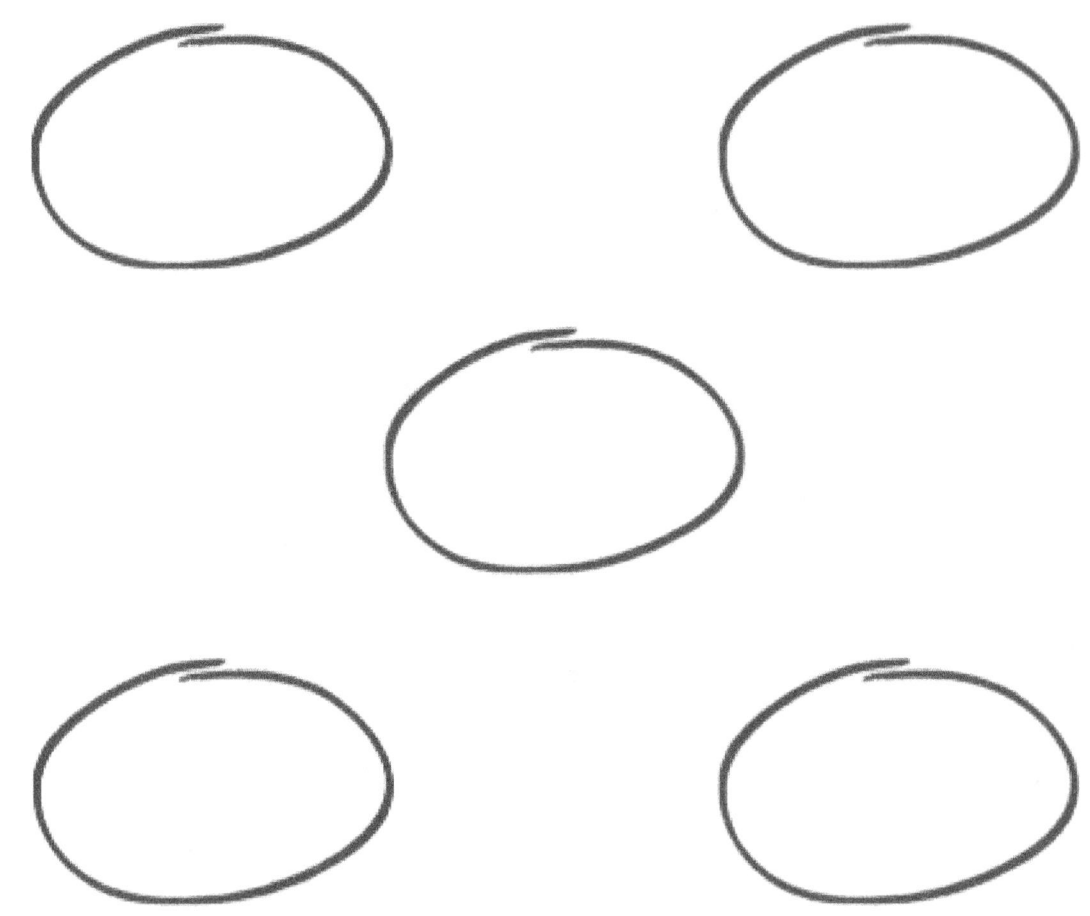

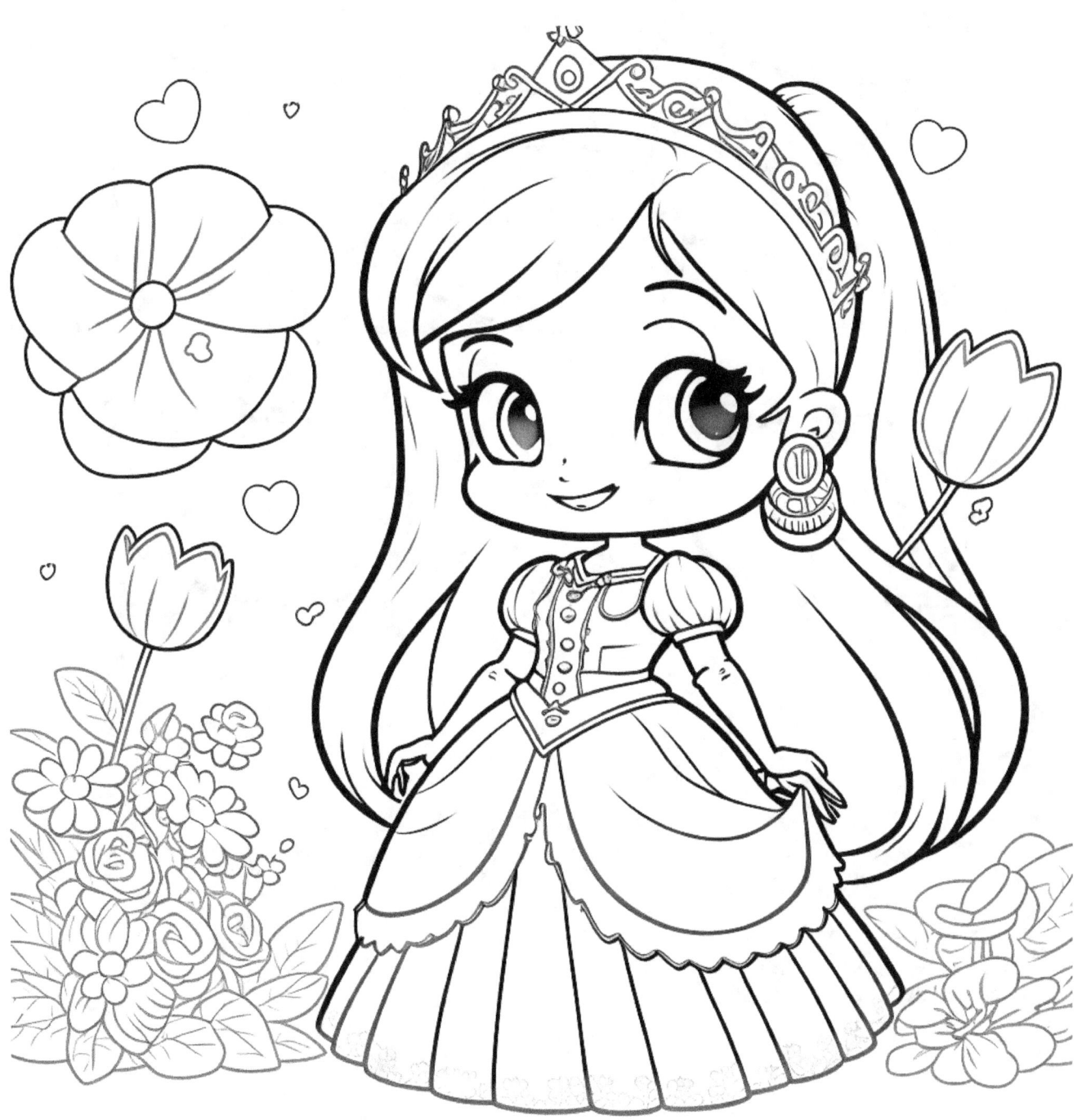

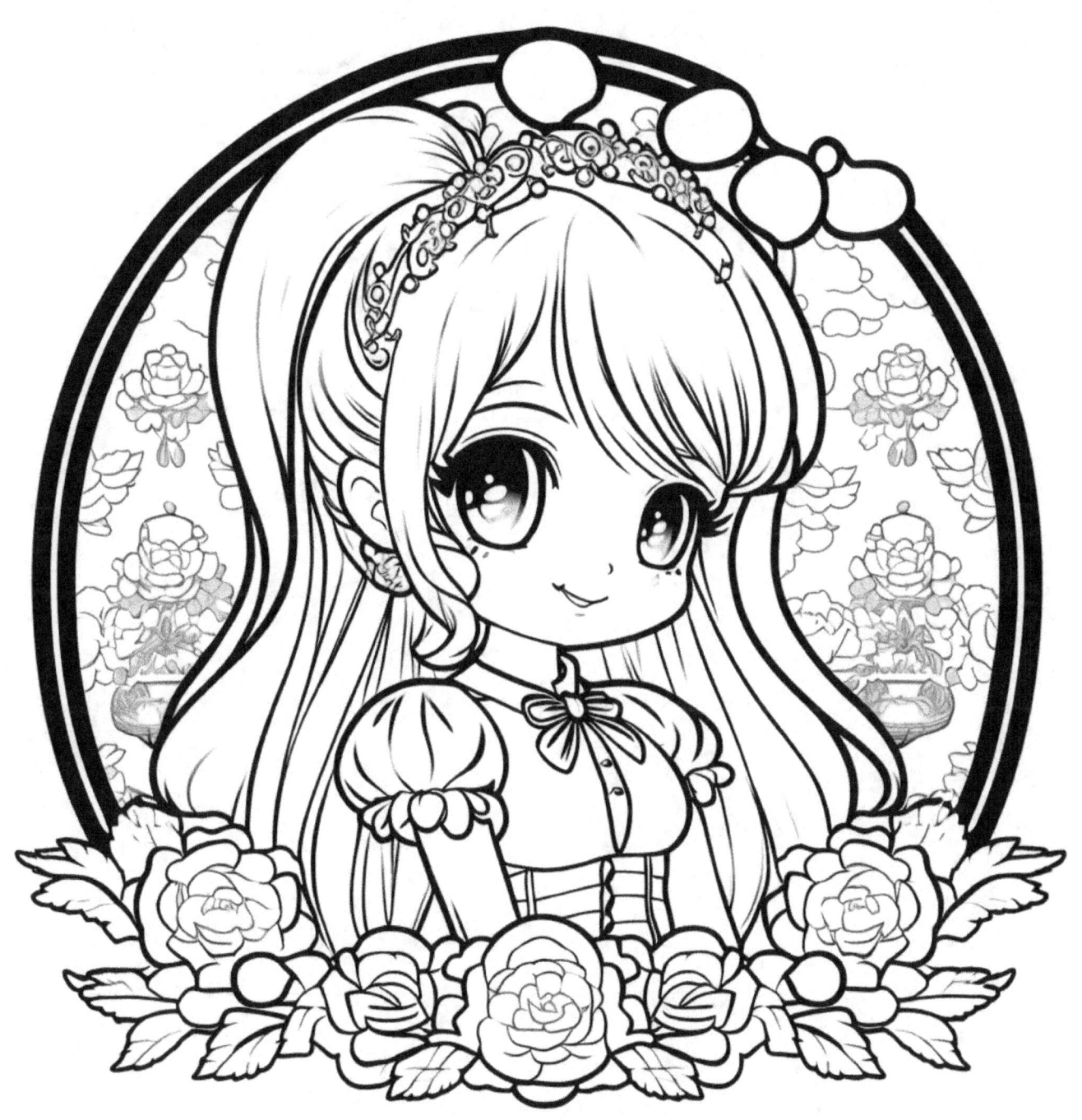

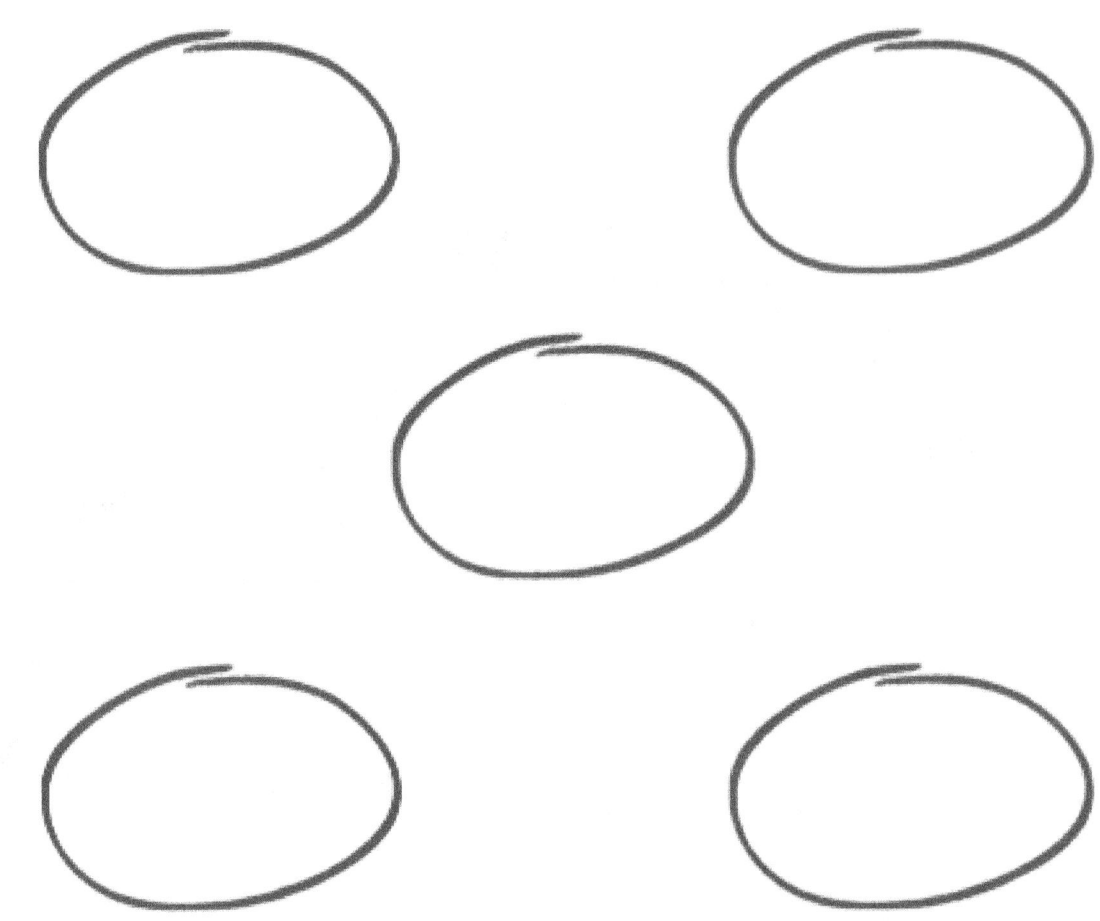

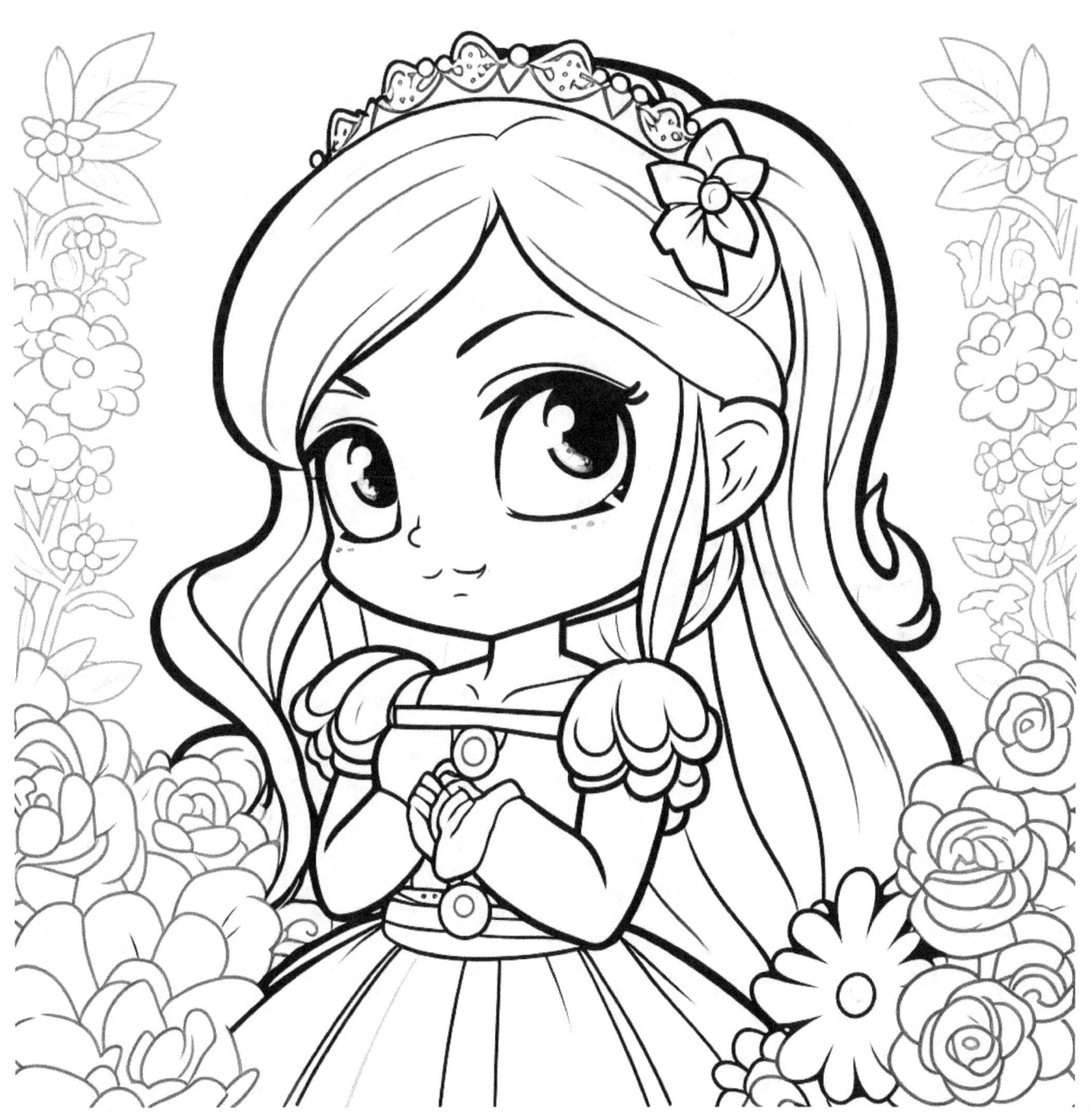

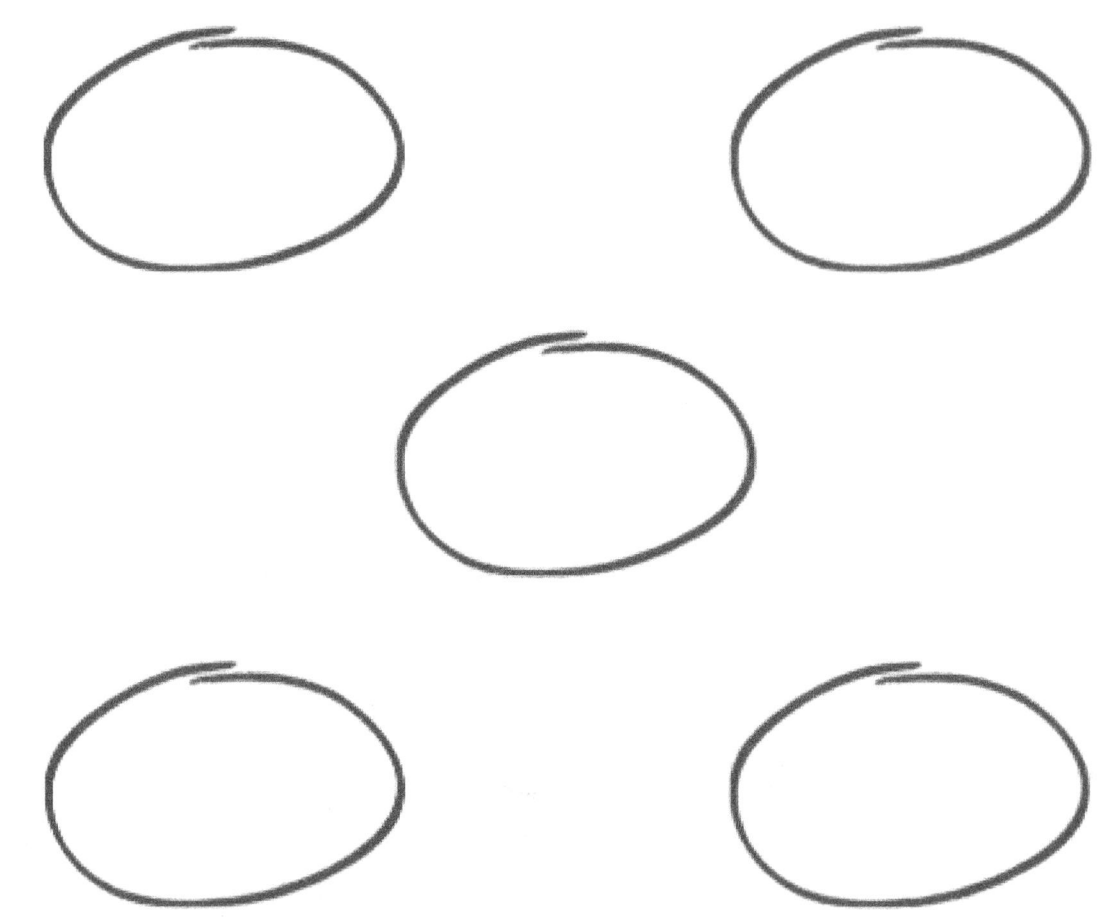

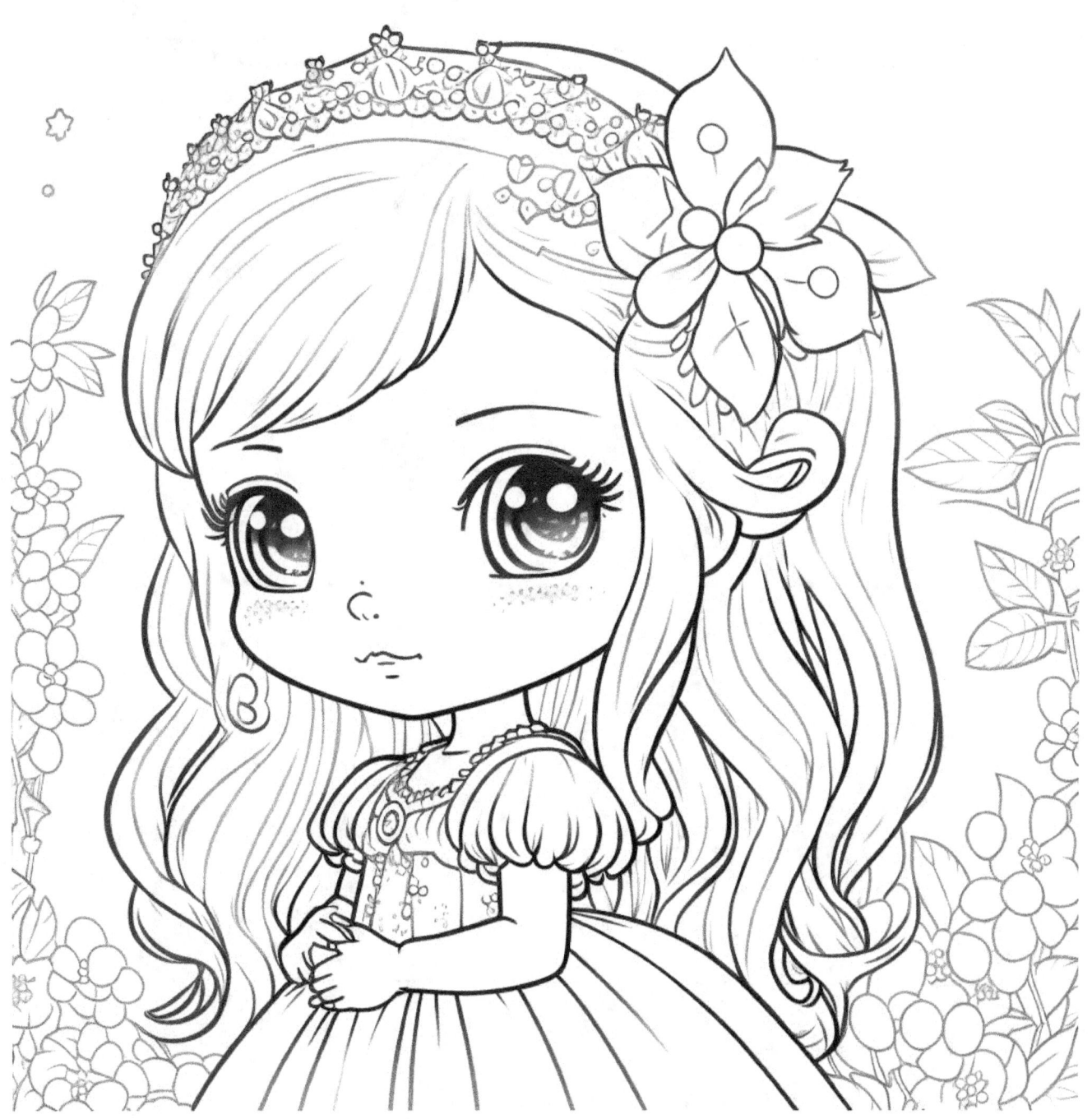

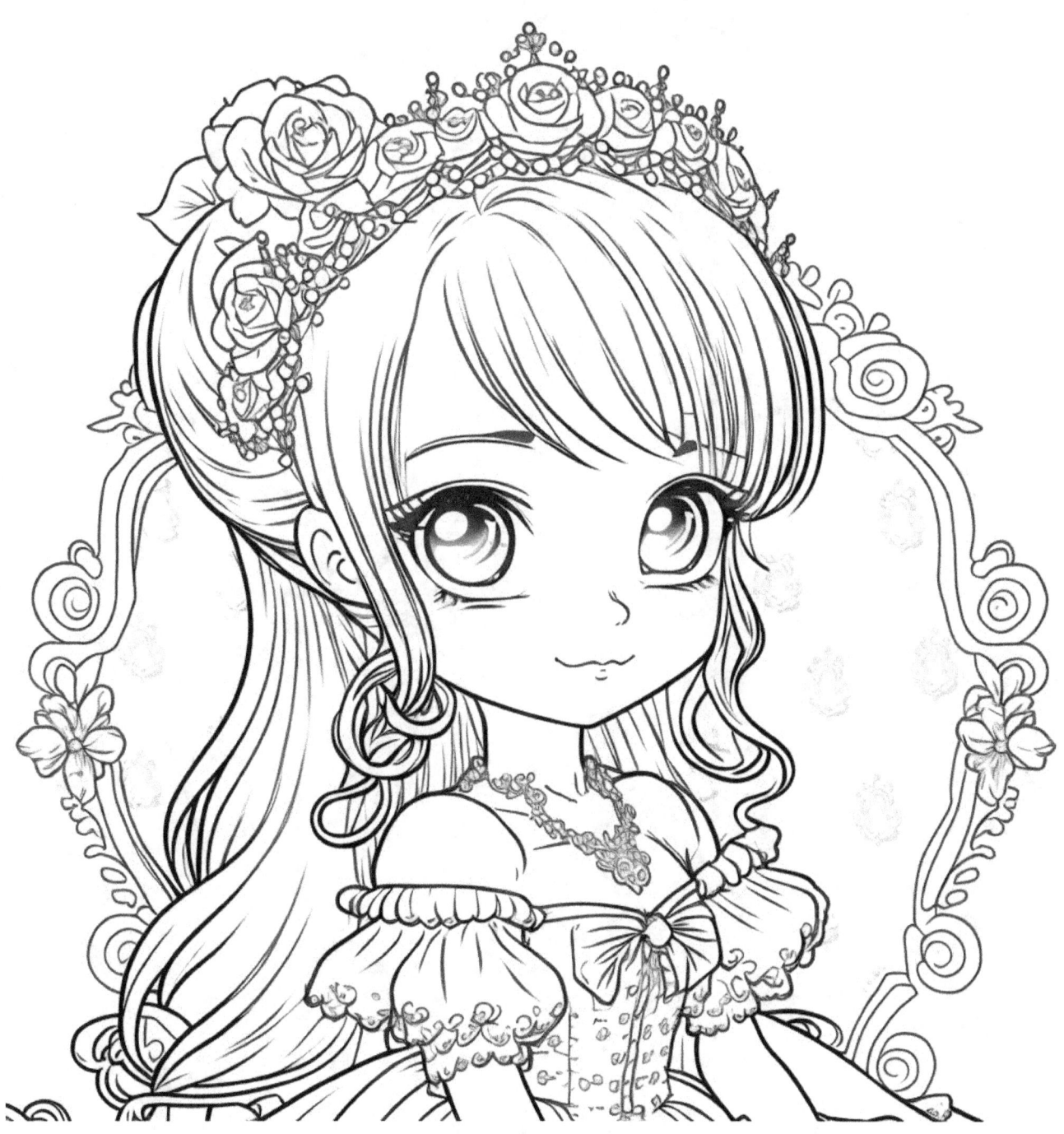

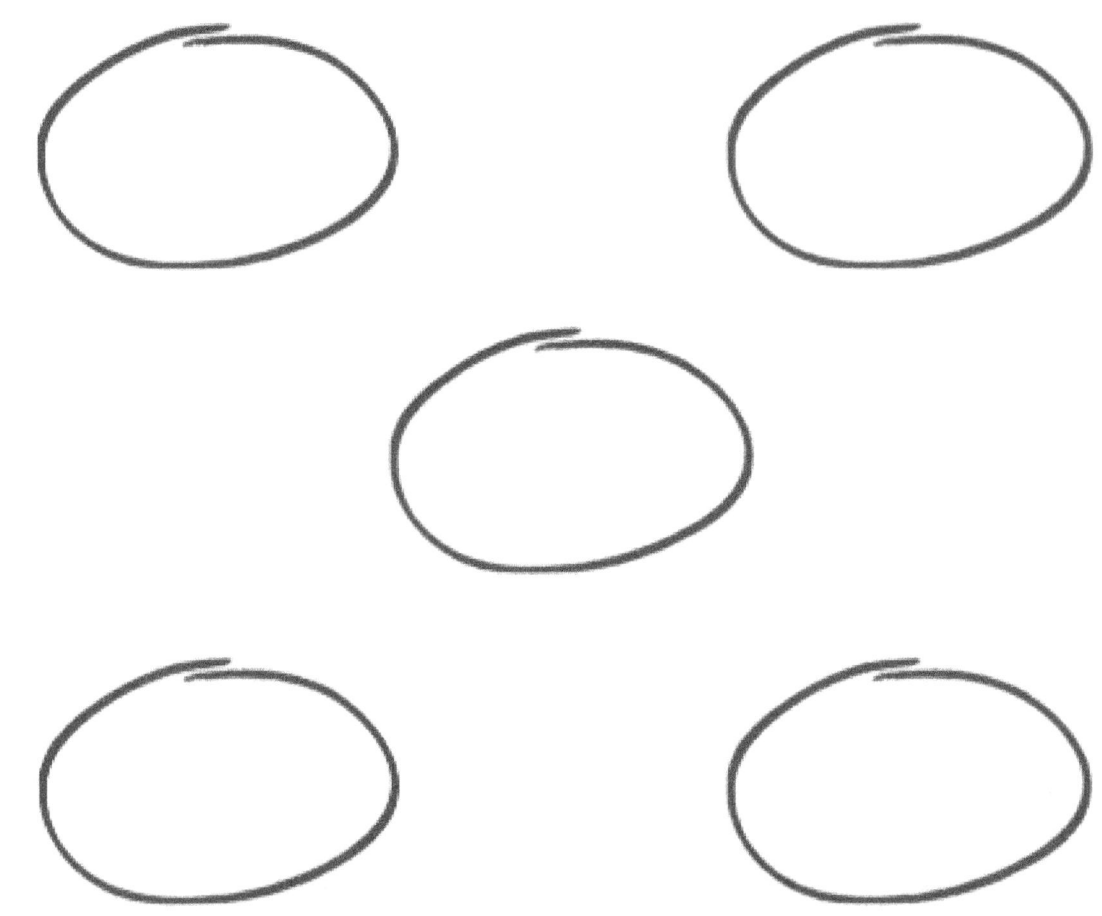

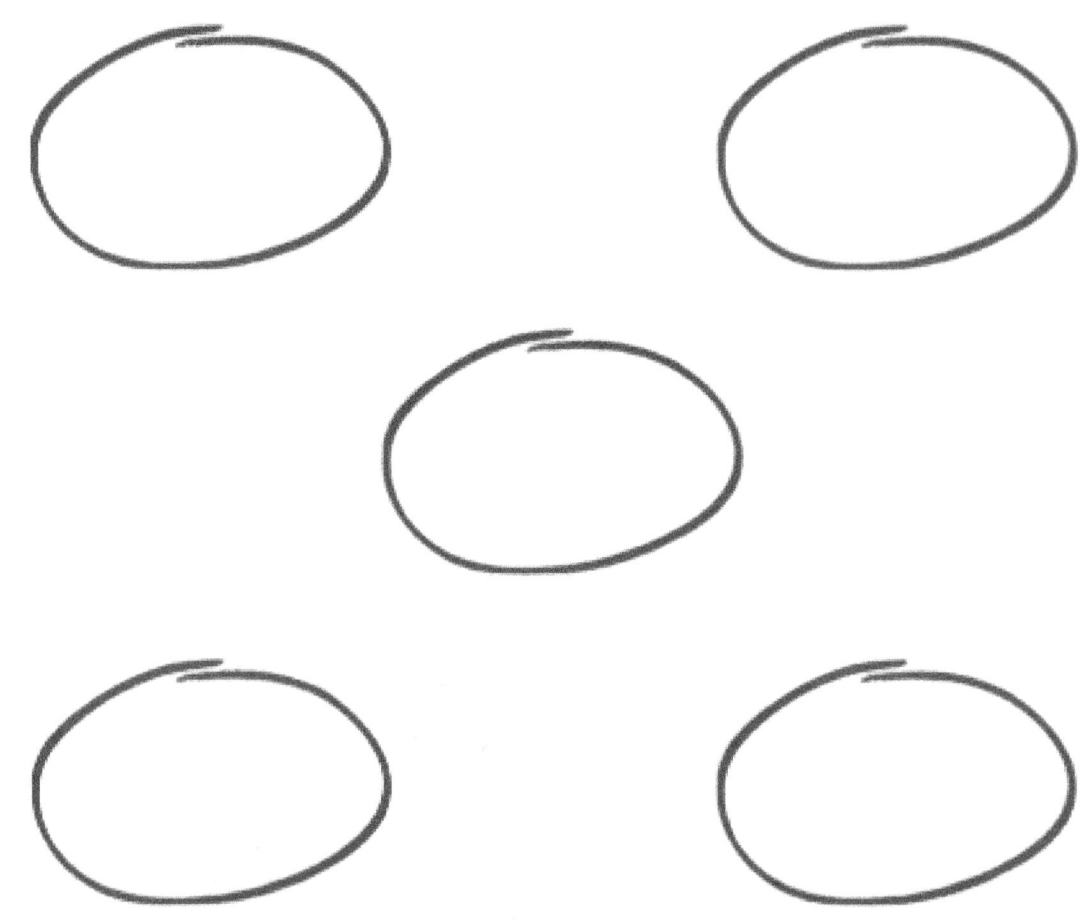

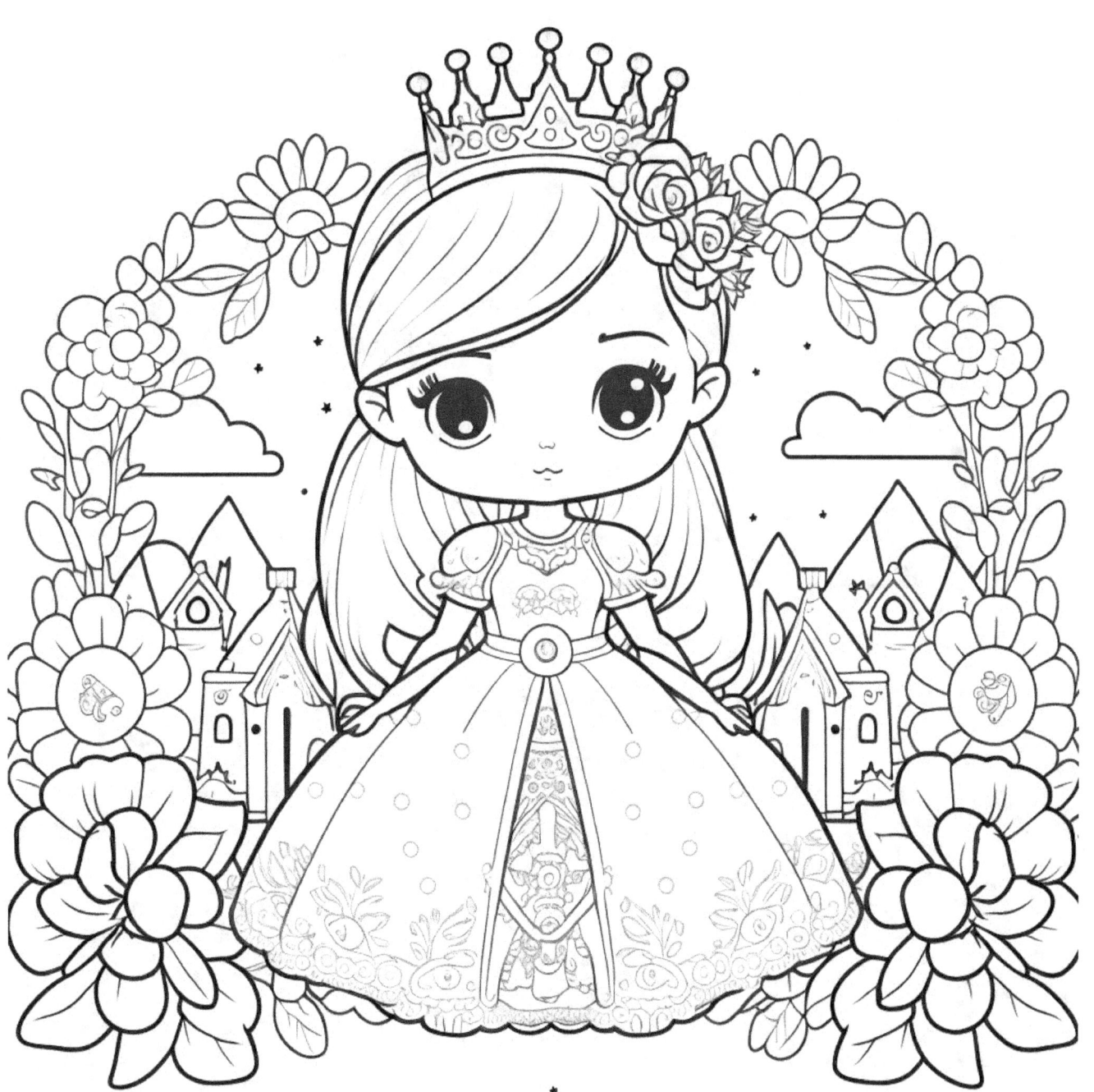

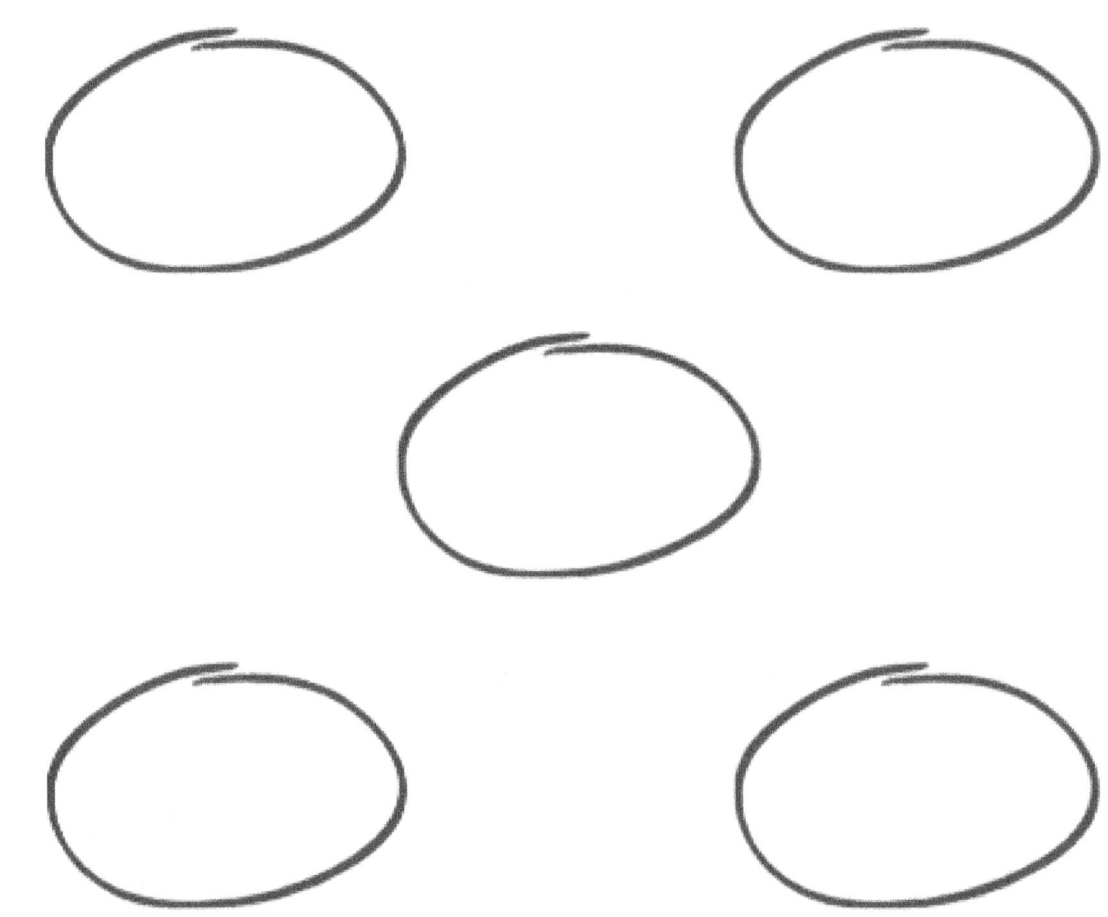

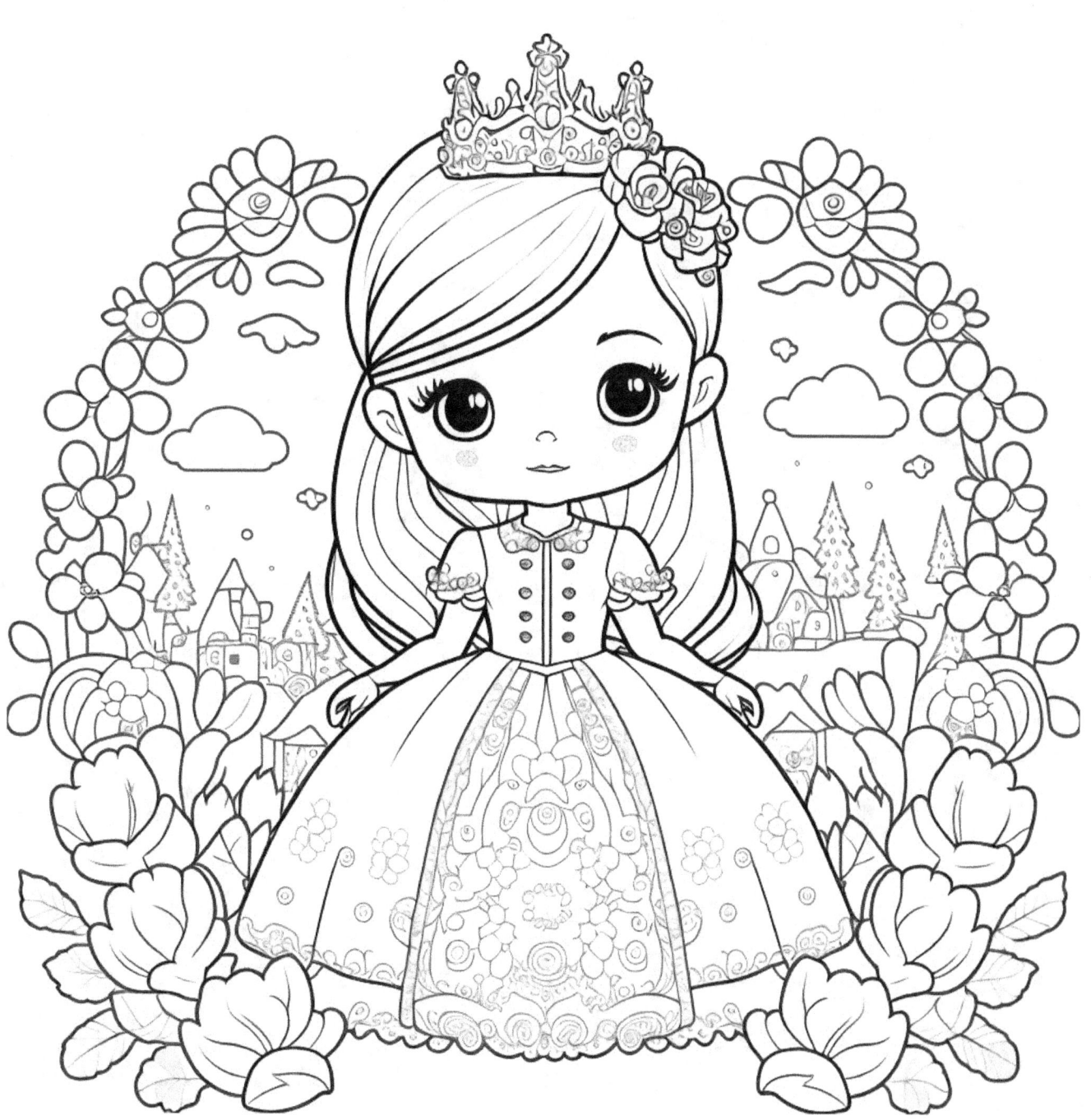

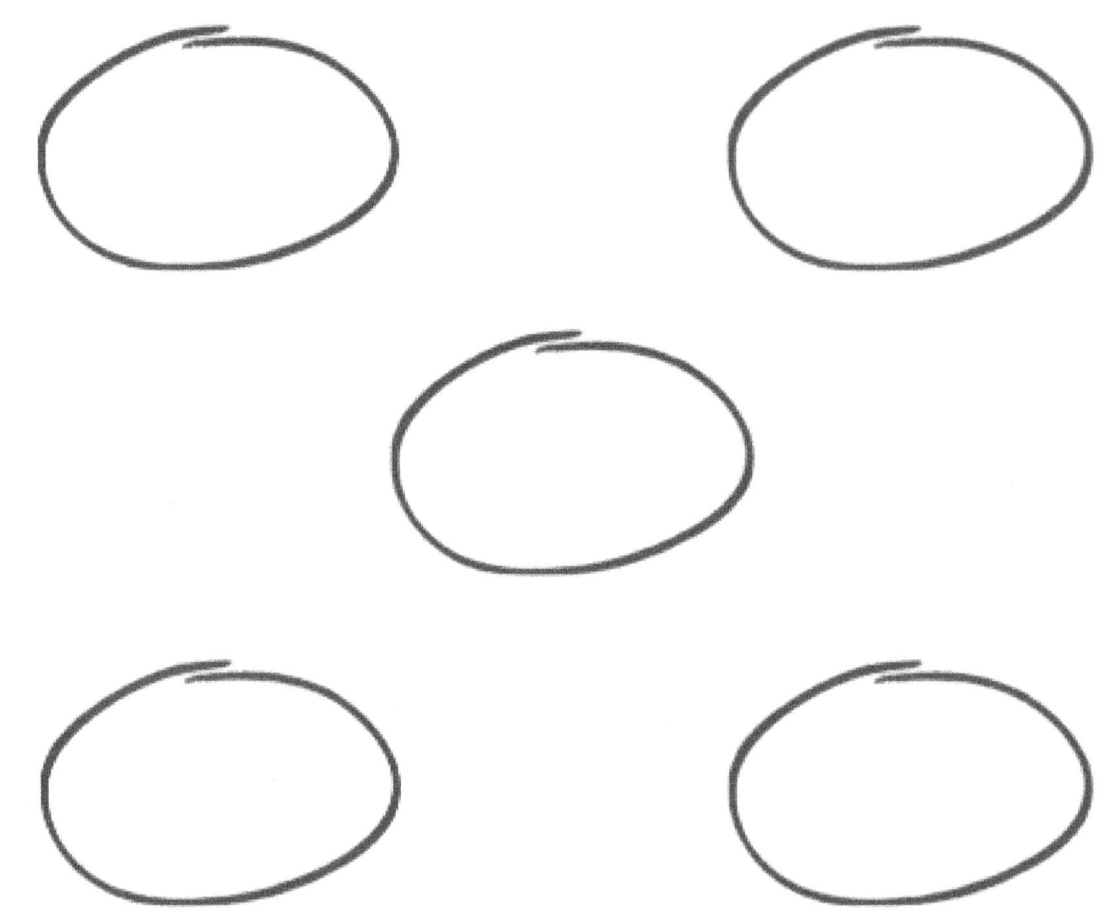

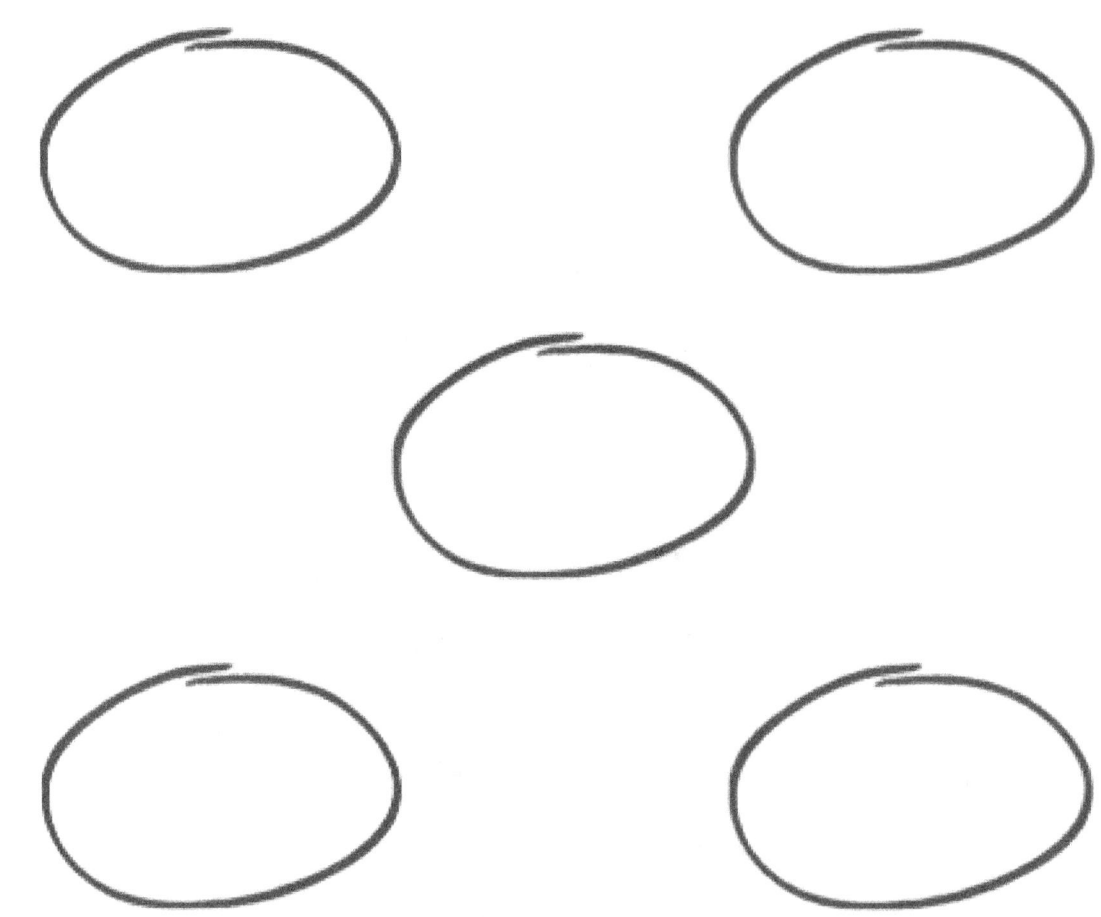

Thank you!

Please check out our other coloring books!

www.ingramcontent.com/pod-product-compliance
Lightning Source LLC
Chambersburg PA
CBHW080851220526
45467CB00008B/2471